Crochet Patterns

GNOMES

Halloween Edition

Recommendations

NOTE: The yarn and tools stated in this section are suitable for all projects from this book (the yarn and tool info for pumpkin projects is stated on the pumpkin project's pages)

YARN

Blend: cotton and acrylic fiber yarn
Yarn Weight: Sport / Fine
Yarn length/weight: approx. 160 meters (174 yds) per 50g ram ball.
Yarn ideas: YarnArt Jeans (used for designs from this book), Scheepjes Softfun, Sirdar Snuggly Replay DK

If you are going to use different from the required yarn, you need to grab a crochet hook that suitable for your yarn and gauge/tension should be tight enough, so the toy stuffing doesn't show up through the crocheted fabric.

TOOLS

Crochet Hook in Metric Size Range: 2.5 mm
Stitch markers x3

GAUGE/TENSION

Rd 1	6SC in magic ring, tighten the ring [6]
Rd 2	INC in each st around [12]
Rd 3	*(SC in next st, INC in next st) from*rep x6 [18]
Rd 4	*(SC in next st, INC in next st, SC in next st) from*rep x6 [24]
Rd 5	*(SC in next 3sts, INC in next st) from*rep x6 [30]
Rd 6	*(SC in next 2sts, INC in next st, SC in next 2sts) from*rep x6 [36]

Size: Ø4.5-5 cm
If you use different yarn, remember that your crocheted fabric should be tight enough, so a filler doesn't show through stitches.

Recommendations

TIPS BEFORE YOU START

Single Crochet "V" and "X"
The typical method to make a single crochet is to insert your hook into a stitch, yarn over, pull through, yarn over, pull through both loops. This method makes a 'V' stitch.
The other lesser-known method to make a single crochet is to insert your hook into a stitch, yarn under, pull through, yarn over, pull through both loops. This method makes an 'X' stitch. Please, note that I use SC "x".

Scan for the
video tutorial

LIFEHACK

You can use this crocheted item as a door stop.
Make a small fabric bag (a size 10cm x 15cm or so) (as well you can use a finished small pouch bag and stitch along an opening when a bag is filled with some filler)
Fill with Pebbles, cat litter, washed sand, rice or beans (food may attract insects)
When you have done a first round with decrease at a bottom of each gnome you can put the bag inside along with the rest of the filler and continue crocheting closing the bottom.

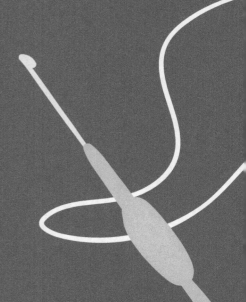

Abbreviations (US terms)

Scan for the
video tutorial

St(s)	Stitch/es
Rd	Round
Ch	Chain stitch

SC	Single Crochet "X"

DC	Double Crochet: yarn over, insert hook in stitch, yarn over, pull through stitch, [yarn over, pull through two loops] twice

sl st	slip stitch: insert hook in stitch, yarn over, pull through both loops on hook

hdc	Half Double Crochet: yarn over, insert in stitch, yarn over, pull through st, yarn over, pull through all 3 loops on hook

TR	Triple crochet: Yarn over the hook 2 times and insert your hook in indicated stitch. Yarn over the hook and pull hook through stitch. Yarn over the hook and draw your yarn through the first 2 loops on your hook. Yarn over the hook and draw your yarn through the next 2 loops on your hook. Yarn over the hook and draw your yarn through the last 2 loops on your hook.

SC2tog	Single crochet two together: Insert hook into stitch and draw up a loop. Insert hook into next stitch and draw up a loop. Yarn over, draw through all 3 loops on hook.

Abbreviations (US terms)

DC2tog	Double crochet two stitches together
INC	Increase: single crochet in one stitch twice
Ch-space	Chain-space
prev	previous
BLO	Back loop only
FLO	Front Loop only
*(...) from*rep x	work instructions within parentheses as many times as directed by x
Surface slip stitch	Place a thread behind the fabric, insert hook into the crocheted fabric from the front to the back and grab yarn on hook, pull a loop through to the front. Insert hook from front to back and pull a loop to the front side and through the loop on the front of the fabric to create a surface slipped stitch.
Bobble st	Work 4 unfinished double crochet in one stitch and complete them all together
FP/BP	

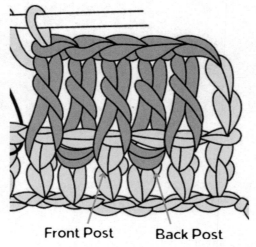

Front Post   **Back Post**

Abbreviations (US terms)

FPdc	Front post double crochet

FPdc2tog	Front post double crochet 2 together (1 decrease)

FPsc	Front post single crochet
FPSC2_tog	Front Post 2 single crochet together (1 decrease): 1. work single crochet from front to back around the post of each of next two stitches and complete them together

Abbreviations (US terms)

BPdc   Back post double crochet

INVISIBLE FINISH FOR OPEN CROCHET EDGES

MAGIC RING

Technique - color changing

COLOR CHANGING

You need to follow the pattern until it is time to switch colors, in the stitch previous to the new color, complete the final yarn over and draw through with the new color you are switching to.

Always change color in the last stitch of a current color completing the last stitch with a new color.

Tapestry crochet: Crochet as usual with the non-working color carried inside the stitch. Places where we need to use the tapestry crochet technique are always stated in the pattern

Scan for the video tutorial

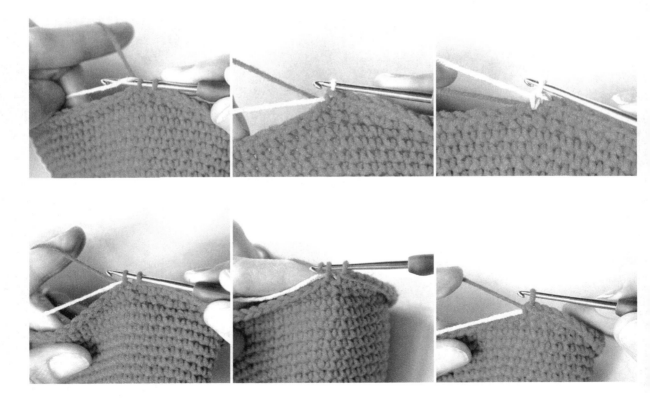

Tips

Twisted Cord.

The initial thread length should be three times longer of the final cord length. For example, if your final cord should be approx. 50 cm, you need to grab 150 cm length threads

1. Use necessary colors(min x2 threads) approx. 150 cm each thread, make a knot on one end
2. Hook on for something (I use door handle) and start to twist. Twist it well
3. Fold in half and remove the end from the door handle
4. Straighten the cord and make a knot on the other end

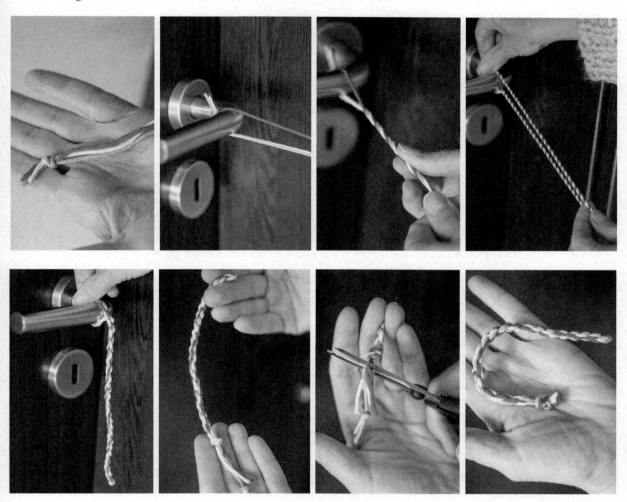

Basic Halloween Gnome

SIZE: 26 cm / 10 in

	YARN BRAND AND COLORS		TOTAL FOR A PROJECT
Black	★	Yarn Art Jeans 28	Approx. 25g\90meters
Pumpkin Orange	★	Yarn Art Jeans 85	Approx. 10g\35meters
Violet	★	Yarn Art Jeans 72	Approx. 20g\70meters
Fog Gray	★	Yarn Art Jeans 49	Approx. 5g\20meters
Light Green	★	Yarn Art Jeans 29	Approx. 3g\10meters
Bright Yellow (for a clasp embroidery)	★	Yarn Art Jeans 35	Approx. 1g

OTHER MATERIALS	CROCHET STICHES	TOOLS
Stuffing approx. 50g	Magic ring, Ch, SC, DC, INC, sl st, SC2tog, FLO, BLO	Crochet hook 2.5 mm

HAT

Use a contrast thread to mark the beginning of each round. Do not remove it until you colplete your work

STEP 1 HAT (work in continuous rounds)

Rd 1	**Black:** 6SC in magic ring [6], tighten the ring
Rd 2	SC in each st around [6]
Rd 3	*(SC in next st, INC in next st) from*rep x3 [9]
Rd 4	SC in each st around [9]
Rd 5	*(SC in next st, INC in next st, SC in next st) from*rep x3 [12]
Rd 6-7	SC in each st around [12]
Rd 8	*(SC in next 3sts, INC in next st)from*repx3 [15]
Rd 9	SC in next 2sts, SC FLO in next 5sts(*), SC in next 8sts [15]
Rd 10	SC in each st around [15]
Rd 11	*(SC in next 2sts, INC in next st, SC in next 2sts) from*rep x3 [18]
Rd 12	SC in next 3sts, SC into next 5sts of prev rd and Rd 8 BLO(*) at the same time(by doing this we gather the hat), SC in next 10sts [18]
Rd 13	SC in each st around [18]
Rd 14	*(SC in next 5sts, INC in next st)from*rep x3 [21]
Rd 15	SC in next 12sts, SC FLO in next 5sts(**), SC in next 4sts [21]
Rd 16	SC in each st around [21]
Rd 17	*(SC in next 3sts, INC in next st, SC in next 3sts) from*rep x3 [24]
Rd 18	SC in next 14sts, SC into next 5sts of prev rd and Rd 14 BLO(**) at the same time(by doing this we gather the hat), SC in next 5sts [24]
Rd 19	SC in each st around [24]
Rd 20	*(SC in next 7sts, INC in next st)from*rep x3 [27]
Rd 21	SC in each st around [27]
Rd 22	SC in next 4sts, SC FLO in next 7sts(***), SC in next 16sts [27]
Rd 23	*(SC in next 4sts, INC in next st, SC in next 4sts) from*rep x3 [30]
Rd 24	SC in each st around [30]

Rd 25	SC in next 5sts, SC into next 7sts of prev rd and Rd 21 BLO(***) at the same time(by doing this we gather the hat), SC in next 18sts [30]
Rd 26	*(SC in next 9sts, INC in next st)from*rep x3 [33]
Rd 27	SC in next 15sts, SC FLO in next 10sts(****), SC in next 8sts [33]
Rd 28	SC in each st around [33]
Rd 29	*(SC in next 5sts, INC in next st, SC in next 5sts) from*rep x3 [36]
Rd 30	SC in next 17sts, SC into next 10sts of prev rd and Rd 26 BLO(****) at the same time, SC in next 9sts [36]
Rd 31	SC in each st around [36]
Rd 32	*(SC in next 11sts, INC in next st)from*rep x3 [39]
Rd 33	SC FLO in each st around [39]
Rd 34	SC in each st around [39]
Rd 35	*(SC in next 6sts, INC in next st, SC in next 6sts) from*rep x3 [42]
Rd 36	*(SC into next 7sts of prev rd and Rd 32 BLO at the same time, SC in next st, SC into next 6sts of prev rd and Rd 32 BLO at the same time) from*rep x3 [42]
Rd 37	SC in each st around [42]
Rd 38	SC FLO in each st around [42]
Rd 39	*(SC in next 13sts, INC in next st) from*rep x3 [45]
Rd 40	SC in each st around [45]
Rd 41	*(SC into next 14sts of prev rd and Rd 37 BLO at the same time, SC in next st)from*rep x3 [45]
Rd 42	SC in each st around [45]
Rd 43	SC FLO in each st around [45]
Rd 44	*(SC in next 7sts, INC in next st, SC in next 7sts) from*rep x3 [48]
Rd 45	SC in each st around [48]
Rd 46	*(SC into next 8sts of prev rd and Rd 42 BLO at the same time, SC in next st, SC into next 7sts of prev rd and Rd 42 BLO at the same time)from*rep x3 [48]
Rd 47-49	SC in each st around [48]

STEP 2 Continue - HAT BRIM (work in continuous rounds)

Rd 50	*(SC FLO in next 5sts, INC FLO in next st)from*rep x8 [56]
Rd 51	*(SC in next 3sts, INC in next st, SC in next 3sts) from*rep x8 [64]
Rd 52	*(SC in next 7sts, INC in next st)from*rep x8 [72]
Rd 53	*(SC in next 4sts, INC in next st, SC in next 4sts) from*rep x8 [80]
Rd 54	SC in each st around [80]
Rd 55	sl st in each st around [80]
	Cut off thread

STEP 3 BODY (work in continuous rounds)

Rd 1-2	Grab the hat upside down, work into available loops (BLO) of Rd 49 with **Violet**: SC BLO in each st around [48]
Rd 3-9	SC in each st around [48]
Rd 10	*(SC in next 7sts, INC in next st)from*rep x6 [54]
Rd 11-13	SC in each st around [54]
Rd 14	*(SC in next 4sts, INC in next st, SC in next 4sts) from*rep x6 [60]
Rd 15-17	SC in each st around [60]
Rd 18	*(SC in next 4sts, SC2tog, SC in next 4sts)from*rep x6 [54]
Rd 19-20	SC in each st around [54]
Rd 21	*(SC in next 7sts, SC2tog)from*rep x6 [48]
Rd 22-23	SC in each st around [48]
Rd 24	SC BLO in each st around [48]
Rd 25	*(SC in next 2sts, SC2tog, SC in next 2sts)from*rep x8 [40]
	Stuff
Rd 26	*(SC in next 3sts, SC2tog) from*rep x8 [32]
Rd 27	*(SC in next st, SC2tog, SC in next st) from*rep x8 [24]
Rd 28	*(SC in next st, SC2tog) from*rep x8 [16]
	Stuff
Rd 29	SC2tog x8 [8]
	Cut off thread. Sew the opening

STEP 3 BODY

STEP 4 HAT DECORATION

 Light Green: Chain 54 [54]

Row 1   DC in 4th st from hook, DC in each st across [52]

Cut off thread leaving a long tail for sewing. Sew the hat decoration on the hat and embroider a clasp with **Yellow**

STEP 5 STAND

Rd 1   Join **Black** to Rd 23 (STEP 3 - Body) and work: Ch1, SC FLO in each st around [48]

BEARD (work in continuous rounds)

	Pumpkin Orange: Chain 2 [2]
Rd 1	3SC in 2nd st from hook [3] (work in the round)
Rd 2	INC in each of next 3SC [6]
Rd 3	INC in each of next 2sts, SC in next 2sts, INC in next st, SC in next st [9]
Rd 4	SC in next st, INC in each of next 2sts, SC in next 5sts, INC in next st [12]
Rd 5	SC in next 2sts, INC in each of next 2sts, SC in next 5sts, INC in next st, SC in next 2sts [15]
Rd 6	SC in next 3sts, INC in each of next 2sts, SC in next 9sts, INC in next st [18]
Rd 7	SC in next 4sts, INC in each of next 2sts, SC in next 8sts, INC in next st, SC in next 3sts [21]
Rd 8	SC in next 5sts, INC in each of next 2sts, SC in next 14sts [23]
Rd 9	SC in next 6sts, INC in each of next 2sts, SC in next 14sts, INC in next st [26]
Rd 10-12	SC in each st around [26]
Rd 13	SC in next 8sts, SC2tog, SC in next 11sts, SC2tog, SC in next 3sts [24]
Rd 14	SC in next 7sts, SC2tog, SC in next 10sts, SC2tog, SC in next 3sts [22]
Rd 15	SC in next 6sts, SC2tog, SC in next 9sts, SC2tog, SC in next 3sts [20]

Cut off thread leaving a long tail for sewing

NOSE (work in continuous rounds)

Rd 1	**Fog grey:** 6SC in magic ring [6] tighten the ring
Rd 2	INC in each st around [12]
Rd 3	*(SC in next st, INC in next st) from*rep x6 [18]
Rd 4-5	SC in each st around [18]
Rd 6	*(SC in next st, SC2tog) from*rep x6 [12]

Cut off thread leaving a long tail for sewing. Stuff the nose a bit and attach to the beard (sew or glue)

ARMs x2 (work in continuous rounds)

STEP 1 PALMS

Rd 1	**Fog Gray:** 5SC in magic ring [5]tighten the ring
Rd 2	INC in each st around [10]
Rd 3-5	SC in each st around [10] Change to Violet in last st. Cut off Fog gray
Rd 6-7	**Violet:** SC in each st around [10]
Rd 8	SC BLO in each st around [10]
Rd 9-17	SC in each st around [10]

Cut off thread leaving a long tail for sewing

STEP 2 CUFF

Rd 1	With **Black** work into available stitch loops (FLO) of 7th rd: SC FLO in each st around [10]
Rd 2-3	SC in each st around [10]

Cut off thread

ARMs STEP 1 -PALMS   **ARMs STEP 2 -CUFF**

Attach the nose with the beard to the body it to the body under the hat brim in front. Attach the arms to the body on sides.

Witch Gnome

SIZE: 26 cm / 10 in

	YARN BRAND AND COLORs		TOTAL FOR A PROJECT
Black	★	Yarn Art Jeans 28	Approx. 15g/50meters
Pumpkin Orange	★	Yarn Art Jeans 85	Approx. 10g/35meters
Violet	★	Yarn Art Jeans 72	Approx. 20g/70meters
White	★	Yarn Art Jeans 62	Approx. 15g/50meters
Light Green	★	Yarn Art Jeans 29	Approx. 7g/25meters
Yellow (for a clasp embroidery)	★	Yarn Art Jeans 35	Approx. 1g

OTHER MATERIALS	CROCHET STICHES	TOOLS
Stuffing approx. 50g	Magic ring, Ch, SC, DC, INC, sl st, SC2tog, FLO, BLO	Crochet hook 2.5 mm

HAT

Use a contrast thread to mark the beginning of each round. Do not remove it until you colplete your work

STEP 1 HAT (work in continuous rounds)

Rd 1	**Violet:** 6SC in magic ring [6] tighten the ring
Rd 2	SC in each st around [6]
Rd 3	*(SC in next st, INC in next st) from*rep x3 [9]
Rd 4	SC in each st around [9]
Rd 5	*(SC in next st, INC in next st, SC in next st) from*rep x3 [12]
Rd 6	SC in each st around [12]
Rd 7	*(SC in next 3sts, INC in next st) from*repx3 [15]
Rd 8	SC in each st around [15]
Rd 9	*(SC in next 2sts, INC in next st, SC in next 2sts) from*rep x3 [18]
Rd 10	SC in each st around [18]
Rd 11	*(SC in next 5sts, INC in next st) from*rep x3 [21]
Rd 12	SC in each st around [21]
Rd 13	*(SC in next 3sts, INC in next st, SC in next 3sts) from*rep x3 [24]
Rd 14	SC in each st around [24]
Rd 15	*(SC in next 7sts, INC in next st) from*rep x3 [27]
Rd 16	SC in each st around [27]
Rd 17	*(SC in next 4sts, INC in next st, SC in next 4sts) from*rep x3 [30]
Rd 18	SC in each st around [30]
Rd 19	*(SC in next 9sts, INC in next st) from*rep x3 [33]
Rd 20	SC in each st around [33]
Rd 21	*(SC in next 5sts, INC in next st, SC in next 5sts) from*rep x3 [36]
Rd 22	SC in each st around [36]
Rd 23	*(SC in next 11sts, INC in next st) from*rep x3 [39]
Rd 24	SC in each st around [39]
Rd 25	*(SC in next 6sts, INC in next st, SC in next 6sts) from*rep x3 [42]
Rd 26	SC in each st around [42]

Rd 27	*(SC in next 13sts, INC in next st) from*rep x3 [45]
Rd 28	SC in each st around [45]
Rd 29	*(SC in next 7sts, INC in next st, SC in next 7sts) from*rep x3 [48]
Rd 30	SC in each st around [48]
Rd 31	*(SC in next 15sts, INC in next st) from*rep x3 [51]
Rd 32	SC in each st around [51]
Rd 33	*(SC in next 8sts, INC in next st, SC in next 8sts) from*rep x3 [54]
Rd 34-35	SC in each st around [54]

STEP 2 Continue –HAT BRIM

Rd 36	*(SC FLO in next 5sts, INC FLO in next st) from*rep x9 [63]
Rd 37	*(SC in next 3sts, INC in next st, SC in next 3sts) from*rep x9 [72]
Rd 38	*(SC in next 4sts, INC in next st, SC in next 4sts) from*rep x8 [80]
Rd 39	*(SC in next 9sts, INC in next st) from*rep x8 [88]
Rd 40	SC in each st around [88]
Rd 41	Sl st in each st around [88]
	Cut off thread

BODY (work in continuous rounds)

Note: When change a yarn cut off if it's stated in a pattern in other cases, drop a yarn and raise when it's needed. Change a color in last stitch

Rd 1-2	Grab a hat upside down, work into stitches BLO of Rd 35 (Hat) with **Black:** SC BLO in each st around [54] Change to White in last st
Rd 3-4	**White:** SC in each st around [54]
Rd 5-6	**Black:** SC in each st around [54]
Rd 7	**White:** *(SC in next 4sts, INC in next st, SC in next 4sts) from*rep x6 [60]
Rd 8	SC in each st around [60]
Rd 9-10	**Black:** SC in each st around [60]
Rd 11	**White:** *(SC in next 14sts, INC in next st) from*rep x4 [64]
Rd 12	SC in each st around [64]
Rd 13-14	**Black:** SC in each st around [64]
Rd 15	**White:** *(SC in next 3sts, SC2tog, SC in next 3sts) from*rep x8 [56]

Rd 16	SC in each st around [56]
Rd 17	**Black:** SC in each st around [56]
Rd 18	*(SC in next 5sts, SC2tog) from*rep x8 [48]
Rd 19-20	**White:** SC in each st around[48] Cut off White
Rd 21	**Black:** SC BLO in each st around [48]
Rd 22	*(SC in next 2sts, SC2tog, SC in next 2sts) from*rep x8 [40]
	Stuff
Rd 23	*(SC in next 3sts, SC2tog) from*rep x8 [32]
Rd 24	*(SC in next st, SC2tog, SC in next st) from*rep x8 [24]
Rd 25	*(SC in next st, SC2tog) from*rep x8[16]
	Stuff
Rd 26	SC2tog x8 [8]
	Cut off thread. Sew the opening

HAT DECORATION

	Black: Chain 56 [56]
Row 1	DC in 4th st from hook, DC in each st to end [54]
	Cut off thread leaving a long tail for sewing. Sew it on the hat
	Embroider a clasp with **Yellow**

STAND

Rd 1	Join Violet to a beginning of Rd 20 of the Body and work: Ch1, SC FLO in each st around [48]
	Cut off thread

ARMs (work in continuous rounds)

Rd 1	**Light Green:** 5SC in magic ring [5] tighten the ring
Rd 2	INC in each st around [10]
Rd 3-5	SC in each st around [10] Change to Violet in last st
	Cut off Light Green
Rd 6-7	**Violet:** SC in each st around[10]. Change to Black in last st
	Cut off Violet
Rd 8	**Black:** SC in each st around [10]
Rd 9-17	SC in each st around [10]
	Cut off thread leaving a long tail for sewing

NOSE (work in continuous rounds)

Rd 1	**Light Green:** 6SC in magic ring [6] tighten the ring
Rd 2	INC in each st around [12]
Rd 3	*(SC in next st, INC in next st) from*rep x6 [18]
Rd 4-5	SC in each st around [18]
Rd 6	*(SC in next st, SC2tog) from*rep x6 [12]
	Cut off thread leaving a long tail for sewing. Stuff the nose a bit

HAIR

1	Chain 15 3SC in 2nd st from hook, 3SC in each of next st to end
2	Chain 15 3SC in 2nd st from hook, 3SC in each of next st to end
3	Chain 15 3SC in 2nd st from hook, 3SC in each of next st to end
	Cut off thread leaving a long tail for sewing

**Sew the nose under the hat brim in front.
Sew the arms under the hat brim on sides.
Sew hair in between the nose and arms
under the hat brim**

Gnome with a long hat

SIZE: 30 cm / 12 in

YARN BRAND AND COLORS			TOTAL FOR A PROJECT
Black	★	Yarn Art Jeans 28	Approx. 10g/35meters
Pumpkin Orange	★	Yarn Art Jeans 85	Approx. 10g/35meters
Violet	★	Yarn Art Jeans 72	Approx. 10g/35meters
White	★	Yarn Art Jeans 62	Approx. 5g/20meters
Light Green	★	Yarn Art Jeans 29	Approx. 7g/25meters
Fog Gray	★	Yarn Art Jeans 49	Approx. 20g/75meters

OTHER MATERIALS	CROCHET STICHES	TOOLS
Stuffing approx. 50g	Magic ring, Ch, SC, DC, INC, sl st, SC2tog, FLO, BLO	Crochet hook 2.5 mm

HAT

Note: Before you start, make a second ball of Black (approx. 5 grams) (or you can use the second end of the ball when it's needed)

Note: Use a contrast thread to mark the beginning of each round. Do not remove it until you colplete your work

Note: When you change a yarn cut it off if it's stated in the pattern, in other cases, drop a yarn and raise it when it's needed

Note: Change to the next color in the last st in the round of the current color

STEP 1 HAT (work in continuous rounds)

Rd 1	**Black:** 6SC in magic ring[6] tighten ring
Rd 2	SC in each st around [6]
Rd 3	**Pumpkin Orange:** *(SC BLO in next st, INC BLO in next st) from*rep x3 [9]
Rd 4	SC in each st around [9]
Rd 5	**Violet:** *(SC BLO in next st, INC BLO in next st, SC BLO in next st) from*rep x3 [12]
Rd 6	SC in each st around [12]
Rd 7	**Black:** SC BLO in each st around [12]
Rd 8	*(SC in next 3sts, INC in next st) from*rep x3 [15]
Rd 9	**Pumpkin Orange:** SC BLO in each st around [15]
Rd 10	SC in each st around [15]
Rd 11	**Violet:** *(SC BLO in next 2sts, INC BLO in next st, SC BLO in next 2sts) from*rep x3 [18]
Rd 12	SC in each st around [18]
Rd 13	**Black:** SC BLO in each st around [18]
Rd 14	*(SC in next 5sts, INC in next st) from*rep x3 [21]
Rd 15	**Pumpkin Orange:** SC BLO in each st around [21]
Rd 16	SC in each st around [21]
Rd 17	**Violet:** *(SC BLO in next 3sts, INC BLO in next st, SC BLO in next 3sts) from*rep x3 [24]
Rd 18	SC in each st around [24]
Rd 19	**Black:** SC BLO in each st around [24]
Rd 20	*(SC in next 7sts, INC in next st) from*rep x3 [27] Change to Pumpkin Orange in last st. Drop a loop from your hook
	Using **Black** from the second ball work surface slip stitch into between Rd 16 and 17. Cut off Black
Rd 21	Grab the dropped loop back on your hook. **Pumpkin Orange:** SC BLO in each st around [27]

Rd 22	SC in each st around [27]
Rd 23	**Violet:** *(SC BLO in next 4sts, INC BLO in next st, SC BLO in next 4sts) from*rep x3 [30]
Rd 24	SC in each st around [30]
Rd 25	**Black:** SC BLO in each st around [30]
Rd 26	*(SC in next 9sts, INC in next st) from*rep x3 [33] Change to Pumpkin Orange in last st. Drop a loop from your hook
	Using **Black** from the second ball work surface slip stitch into between Rd 22 and 23. Cut off Black
Rd 27	Grab the dropped loop back on your hook. **Pumpkin Orange:** SC BLO in each st around [33]
Rd 28	SC in each st around [33]
Rd 29	**Violet:** *(SC BLO in next 5sts, INC BLO in next st, SC BLO in next 5sts) from*rep x3 [36]
Rd 30	SC in each st around [36]
Rd 31	**Black:** SC BLO in each st around [36]
Rd 32	*(SC in next 11sts, INC in next st) from*rep x3 [39] Change to Pumpkin Orange in last st. Drop a loop from your hook
	Using **Black** from the second ball work surface slip stitch into between Rd 28 and 29. Cut off Black
Rd 33	Grab the dropped loop back on your hook. **Pumpkin Orange:** SC BLO in each st around [39]
Rd 34	SC in each st around [39]
Rd 35	**Violet:** *(SC BLO in next 6sts, INC BLO in next st, SC BLO in next 6sts) from*rep x3 [42]
Rd 36	SC in each st around [42]
Rd 37	**Black:** SC BLO in each st around[42]
Rd 38	*(SC in next 13sts, INC in next st) from*rep x3 [45] Change to Pumpkin Orange in last st. Drop a loop from your hook
	Using **Black** from the second ball work surface slip stitch into between Rd 34 and 35. Cut off Black
Rd 39	Grab the dropped loop back on your hook. **Pumpkin Orange:** SC BLO in each st around [45]
Rd 40	SC in each st around [45]
Rd 41	**Violet:** *(SC BLO in next 7sts, INC BLO in next st, SC BLO in next 7sts) from*rep x3 [48]
Rd 42	SC in each st around [48]
Rd 43	**Black:** SC BLO in each st around [48]

Rd 44	*(SC in next 11sts, INC in next st) from*rep x4 [52] Change to Pumpkin Orange in last st. Drop a loop from your hook
	Using **Black** from the second ball work surface slip stitch into between Rd 40 and 41. Cut off Black
Rd 45	Grab the dropped loop back on your hook. **Pumpkin Orange:** SC BLO in each st around [52]
Rd 46	SC in each st around [52]
Rd 47	**Violet:** *(SC BLO in next 6sts, INC BLO in next st, SC BLO in next 6sts) from*rep x4 [56]
Rd 48	SC in each st around [56]

STEP 2 Continue - HAT BRIM (work in continuous rounds)

Rd 49	**Black:** SC FLO in each st around [56] Drop a loop from your hook
	Using **Black** from the second ball work surface slip stitch into between Rd 46 and 47. Cut off Black
Rd 50	Grab the dropped loop back on your hook. *(SC in next 3sts, INC in next st, SC in next 3sts) from*rep x8 [64]. Change to Pumpkin Orange in last st. Cut off Black
Rd 51	**Pumpkin Orange:** *(SC BLO in next 7sts, INC BLO in next st) from*rep x8 [72]
Rd 52	*(SC in next 4sts, INC in next st, SC in next 4sts) from*rep x8 [80] Change to Violet in last st. Cut off Pumpkin Orange
Rd 53	**Violet:** SC BLO in each st around [80]
Rd 54	sl st in each st around [80] Cut off Violet

BODY (work in continuous rounds)

Rd 1-2	Grab a hat upside down, work into stitches BLO of Rd 48 with **Fog gray:** SC BLO in each st around [56]
Rd 3-6	SC in each st around [56]
Rd 7	*(SC in next 13sts, INC in next st) from*rep x4 [60]
Rd 8-10	SC in each st around [60]
Rd 11	*(SC in next 7sts, INC in next st, SC in next 7sts) from*rep x4 [64]
Rd 12-13	SC in each st around [64]
Rd 14	*(SC in next 3sts, SC2tog, SC in next 3sts) from*rep x8 [56]
Rd 15-17	SC in each st around [56]

	Stuff
Rd 18	*(SC in next 5sts, SC2tog) from*rep x8 [48]
Rd 19-20	SC in each st around [48]
Rd 21	SC BLO in each st around [48]
Rd 22	*(SC in next 2sts, SC2tog, SC in next 2sts) from*rep x8 [40]
	Stuff
Rd 23	*(SC in next 3sts, SC2tog) from*rep x8 [32]
Rd 24	*(SC in next st, SC2tog, SC in next st) from*rep x8 [24]
Rd 25	*(SC in next st, SC2tog) from*rep x8 [16]
	Stuff
Rd 26	SC2tog x8 [8]
	Cut off thread. Sew the opening

STAND

Rd 1	Join **Black** to Rd 20 (Body) and work: Ch1, SC FLO in each st around [48]
	Cut off thread. Fasten off

ARMs (work in continuous rounds)

STEP 1 PALMS

Rd 1	**White**: 5SC in magic ring[5] tighten ring
Rd 2	INC in each st around [10]
Rd 3-5	SC in each st around [10] Change to Fog gray in last st. Cut off White
Rd 6-7	**Fog gray:** SC in each st around [10]
Rd 8	SC BLO in each st around[10]
Rd 9-17	SC in each st around [10]
	Cut off thread leaving a long tail for sewing

STEP 2 CUFF

Rd 1	Join **Black**, work into stitch FLO of Rd 7: SC FLO in each st around [10]
Rd 2-3	SC in each st around [10]
	Cut off thread

BEARD (work in continuous rounds)

	Light green: Chain 2 [2]
Rd 1	3SC in 2nd st from hook [3] (work in the round)
Rd 2	INC in each of next 3SC [6]
Rd 3	INC in each of next 2sts, SC in next 2sts, INC in next st, SC in next st [9]
Rd 4	SC in next st, INC in each of next 2sts, SC in next 5sts, INC in next st [12]
Rd 5	SC in next 2sts, INC in each of next 2sts, SC in next 5sts, INC in next st, SC in next 2sts [15]
Rd 6	SC in next 3sts, INC in each of next 2sts, SC in next 9sts, INC in next st [18]
Rd 7	SC in next 4sts, INC in each of next 2sts, SC in next 8sts, INC in next st, SC in next 3sts [21]
Rd 8	SC in next 5sts, INC in each of next 2sts, SC in next 14sts [23]
Rd 9	SC in next 6sts, INC in each of next 2sts, SC in next 14sts, INC in next st [26]
Rd 10-12	SC in each st around [26]
Rd 13	SC in next 8sts, SC2tog, SC in next 11sts, SC2tog, SC in next 3sts [24]
Rd 14	SC in next 7sts, SC2tog, SC in next 10sts, SC2tog, SC in next 3sts [22]
Rd 15	SC in next 6sts, SC2tog, SC in next 9sts, SC2tog, SC in next 3sts [20]

Cut off thread leaving a long tail for sewing

NOSE (work in continuous rounds)

Rd 1	**White:** 6SC in magic ring[6] tighten ring
Rd 2	INC in each st around [12]
Rd 3	*(SC in next st, INC in next st) from*rep x6 [18]
Rd 4-5	SC in each st around [18]
Rd 6	*(SC in next st, SC2tog) from*rep x6 [12]

Cut off thread leaving a long tail for sewing. Stuff the nose a bit. Attach the nose to the beard (sew/glue)

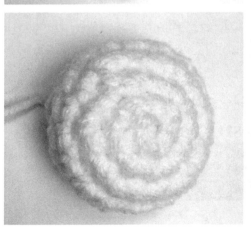

Sew the nose with the beard under the hat brim in front.
Sew the arms under the hat brim on sides.

ADDITIONAL COLOR

MAIN COLOR

Small bobble pumpkin

YOU CAN USE ANY WOOL YARN FROM YOUR STASH, ANY COLORS, AND ANY TEXTURES.

YARN	BRAND AND COLOR CODE	TOTAL FOR PROJECT	HOOK SIZE
Main color	MEDIUM (4) Yarn Impeccable col. Golden Beige (260 m in 128 g)	Approx. 33 g/70 meters	4 mm
Additional color	MEDIUM (4) Yarn Impeccable col. Fern	Approx. 5 g	4 mm
Toy stuffing		Approx. 20 grams	

ADDITIONAL COLOR

MAIN COLOR

Large bobble pumpkin

YARN	BRAND AND COLOR CODE	TOTAL FOR PROJECT	HOOK SIZE
Main color	Super Bulky (6) Alize superlana megafil col. 488 (55 m in 100 g)	Approx. 200 g/110 meters	10 mm
Additional color	Bulky(5) Alize superlana maxi col. 620 (100 m in 100 g)	Approx. 6 g/6 meters	6 mm
Toy stuffing		Approx. 20 grams	

STEP 1 MAIN PART - ribs. Main color

Chain 18

Row 1 [Right side]

sl st in 2nd st from hook, sl st in next st, hdc in next 13sts, sl st in next 2sts, Ch 1 [17]

Row 2 [Wrong side]

sl st BLO in next 2sts, SC in next st, *(BOBBLE in next st, SC in next st) from*rep to last 2sts, sl st BLO in next 2sts, Ch1 [17]

Row 3

sl st BLO in next 2sts, hdc in next 13sts, sl st BLO in next 2sts, Ch1 [17]

Row 4

sl st BLO in next 2sts, SC BLO in next 13sts, sl st BLO in next 2sts, Ch1 [17]

Row 5

sl st BLO in next 2sts, hdc FLO in next 13sts, sl st BLO in next 2sts, Ch1 [17]

Row 6-41

Repeat the pattern Row 2-5 x9 more times [17], You can make your pumpkin of different sizes by doing a different number of repetitions

PENULTIMATE ROW (42)

sl st BLO in next 2sts, SC in next st, *(BOOBLE in next st, SC in next st) from*rep to last 2sts, sl st BLO in next 2sts, Ch1 [17]

LAST ROW (43)

sl st BLO in next 2sts, hdc in next 13sts, sl st BLO in next 2sts, Ch1

Sitch short edges together on Wrong Side by SC. [17] Cut off thread leaving a long tail for sewing

STEP 2 BLOSSOM END. Main color

Rd 1	6SC in magic ring [6]
Rd 2	INC in each st around [12]
Rd 3	*(SC in next st, INC in next st) from*rep x6 [18]
Rd 4	*(SC in next sts, INC in next st, SC in next sts) from*rep x6 [24]
Rd 5	*(SC in next 3sts, INC in next st) from*rep x6 [30]

Cut off thread leaving a long tail for sewing. Attach it to one of the openings with a running stitch

WATCH VIDEO TUTORIAL:
https://youtu.be/4Q8YPm9ZYPI

STEP 2 STEM. Additional color

Make an i-cord of 4 stitches about 3cm length or any desired length. Don't cut off thread and continue:

Rd 1	Drop loops 2, 3, 4 off the hook and hold on them. Work a chain stitch into 1st stitch on your hook, then **work SC into a bar between loops, pull the 2nd loop back on your hook and work SC in this loop**. [7] Work this way** to end until no dropped loops left and work last SC into a bar between loops at the end
Rd 2	INC in each of next 7sts [14]
Rd 3	*(SC in next st, INC in next st) from*rep x7 [21]

ASSEMBLE:

By tapestry needle and yarn tail work whip stitches into slip stitches of one of two opening on the main part(ribs) and tighten it to make the same diameter as the stem. Stitch the stem to the pumpkin opening with a running stitch. Fasten off

WATCH VIDEO TUTORIAL:
https://youtu.be/JtkhqxDl4PA

SCAN ME

40

Pumpkin gnome

SIZE: 26 cm / 10 in

	YARN BRAND AND COLORs		TOTAL FOR A PROJECT
Black	★	Yarn Art Jeans 28	Approx. 26g\100 meters
Pumpkin Orange	★	Yarn Art Jeans 85	Approx. 35g\130 meters
Grass Green	★	Yarn Art Jeans 69	Approx. 2g\7 meters
Honey Caramel	★	Yarn Art Jeans 07	Approx. 5g\20 meters
Mustard (for a cord)	★	Yarn Art Jeans 84	Approx. 0.5 g

OTHER MATERIALS	CROCHET STICHES	TOOLS
Stuffing approx. 40g	Magic ring, Ch, SC, DC, INC, sl st, SC2tog, FP/BP, FPdc2tog FLO, BLO	Crochet hook 2.5 mm

Use a contrast thread to mark the beginning of each round. Do not remove it until you colplete your work

STEP 1 HAT (work in continuous rounds)

Rd 1	**Black:** 6SC in magic ring[6], tighten the ring
Rd 2	INC in each st around [12]
Rd 3	*(SC in next st, INC in next st) from*rep x6 [18]
Rd 4	*(SC in next st, INC in next st, SC in next st) from*rep x6 [24]
Rd 5	*(SC in next 3sts, INC in next st) from*rep x6 [30]
Rd 6	*(SC in next 2sts, INC in next st, SC in next 2sts) from*rep x6 [36]
Rd 7	*(SC in next 5sts, INC in next st) from*rep x6 [42]
Rd 8	*(SC in next 3sts, INC in next st, SC in next 3sts) from*rep x6 [48]
Rd 9	*(SC in next 7sts, INC in next st) from*rep x6 [54]
Rd 10	SC BLO in each st around [54]
Rd 11-18	SC in each st around [54]
Rd 19	SC in next 10 sts, SC FLO in next 12 sts(*), SC in each stitch to end [54]
Rd 20-22	SC in each st around [54]
Rd 23	SC in next 10sts, SC into 12 stitches of prev rd and rd 18 BLO (*) together (by doing this we gather the hat) (pic 1), SC in each stitch to end [54]
Rd 24	SC in next 10sts, SC FLO in next 14sts(**), SC in each stitch to end [54] (pic 2)
Rd 25-26	SC in each st around [54]
Rd 27	SC in next 10sts, SC into 14 stitches of prev rd and rd 23 BLO(**) together (by doing this we gather the hat second time), SC in each stitch to end (pic 3) [54]
Rd 28	SC in next 8sts, SC2tog, SC FLO in next 16sts(***), SC2tog, SC in next 16sts, SC2tog, SC in next 8sts [51]
Rd 29-30	SC in each st around [51]
Rd 31	SC in next 9sts, SC into 16 stitches of prev rd and rd 27 BLO (***) together (by doing this we gather the hat third time), SC in each stitch to end [51] (pic 4)
Rd 32	*(SC in next 15sts, SC2tog) from*rep x3 [48]
Rd 33-34	SC in each st around [48]

STEP 2 Continue – HAT BRIM (work in continuous rounds)

Rd 35	*(SC FLO in next 7sts, INC FLO in next st) from*rep x6 [54]
Rd 36	*(SC in next 4sts, INC in next st, SC in next 4sts) from*rep x6 [60]
Rd 37	*(SC in next 9sts, INC in next st) from*rep x6 [66]
Rd 38	*(SC in next 5sts, INC in next st, SC in next 5sts) from*rep x6 [72]
Rd 39	*(SC in next 11sts, INC in next st) from*rep x6 [78]
Rd 40	Sl st in each st around [78] Cut off thread

BODY (work in joined rounds)

Rd 1-2	Grab a hat upside down, work into stitches BLO of Rd 34 with **Pumpkin Orange: Ch1,** SC BLO in each st around to last st, sl st in 1st stitch [48]
Rd 3	Ch2, DC in each st around to last st, sl st in 2nd Ch [48]
Rd 4-5	Ch2, *(FPdc in next 3sts, BPdc in next st) from*rep x11, FPdc in next 3sts, sl st in 2nd Ch [48]
Rd 6	Ch2, *(FPdc in next sts, 2FPdc in next sts, FPdc in next sts, BPdc in next st, FPdc in next 3sts, BPdc in next st) from*rep x6, sl st in 2nd Ch [55]
Rd 7-8	Ch2, *(FPdc in next 4sts, BPdc in next st, FPdc in next 3sts, BPdc in next st) from*rep x6, sl st in 2nd Ch [55]
Rd 9	Ch2, *(FPdc in next 4sts, BPdc in next st, FPdc in next sts, 2FPdc in next sts, FPdc in next sts, BPdc in next st) from*rep x6, sl st in 2nd Ch [61]
Rd 10-12	Ch2, *(FPdc in next 4sts, BPdc in next st) from*rep x12, sl st in 2nd Ch [61]
Rd 13	Ch2, *(FPdc in next 4sts, 2BPdc in next st) from*rep x12, sl st in 2nd Ch [73]
Rd 14-16	Ch2, *(FPdc in next 4sts, BPdc in next 2sts) from*rep x12, sl st in 2nd Ch [73]
Rd 17	Ch2, *(FPdc in next sts, FPdc2tog, FPdc in next sts, BPdc in next 2sts) from*rep x12, sl st in 2nd Ch [61]

Work in continuous rounds (without joining)

Rd 18	SC BLO in each st around [61]
Rd 19	*(SC in next 10sts, SC2tog) from*rep x5, SC in next st [56]
Rd 20	*(SC in next 5sts, SC2tog) from*rep x8 [48]
Rd 21	*(SC in next 2sts, SC2tog, SC in next 2sts) from*rep x8 [40]

Stuff the gnome a bit. It should not be stuffed firmly

Rd 22	*(SC in next 3sts, SC2tog) from*rep x8 [32]
Rd 23	*(SC in next st, SC2tog, SC in next ts) from*rep x8 [24]
Rd 24	*(SC in next st, SC2tog) from*rep x8 [16]
Rd 25	SC2tog x8 [8]

Cut off thread and sew the opening

ARMs (work in continuous rounds)

STEP 1 PALMS

Rd 1	**Honey Caramel:** 5SC in magic ring [5] tighten the ring
Rd 2	INC in each st around [10]
Rd 3-5	SC in each st around [10] Change to Pumpkin Orange in last st. Cut off Honey Caramel
Rd 6-7	**Pumpkin Orange:** SC in each st around [10]
Rd 8	SC BLO in each st around [10]
Rd 9-17	SC in each st around [10]

Cut off thread leaving a long tail for sewing

STEP 2 CUFF

Rd 1	**Light green** work into stitch FLO of Rd 7: SC FLO in each st around [10]
Rd 2	SC in each st around [10]

Cut off thread

NOSE (work in continuous rounds)

Rd 1	**Honey Caramel:** 6SC in magic ring [6] tighten the ring
Rd 2	INC in each st around [12]
Rd 3	*(SC in next st, INC in next st) from*rep x6 [18]
Rd 4	*(SC in next st, INC in next st, SC in next st) from*rep x6 [24]
Rd 5-6	SC in each st around [24]
Rd 7	*(SC in next st, SC2tog) from*rep x8[16]

Cut off thread leaving a long tail for sewing. Stuff the nose a bit

Sew or glue the nose on the body under the hat brim in front. Attach the arms to the body under the had brim on sides.

Decorate the hat with a twisted cord made with Green and Mustard (see Tips on page 13)

Pumpkin

YARN:

I used some old wool yarn from my stash:
Yarn weight: 4 ply, fingering
Yarn length/weight: 200 meters per 50 g
You need 2 colors: the main color (I used a terracotta color; it can be any color you like) and a green color to make a stem.

Total meters of the main color for this project: approx. 150 meters
Total meters of the green color for this project: approx. 15 meters

OTHER MATERIALS	CROCHET STICHES	TOOLS
Stuffing approx. 40g	Magic ring, Ch, SC, INC, sl st, SC2tog, FP/BP, FPdc2tog, DC2tog	Crochet Hook 3 mm or 3.5 mm

STEP 1 MAIN PART – RIBS.

Main color, work in double strand in case of using the same yarn weight as I do

	Till Rd 4 crochet in continuous rounds
Rd 1	6SC in magic ring [6] tighten the ring
Rd 2	INC in each st around [12]
Rd 3	*(SC in next st, INC in next st) from*rep x6 [18]
Rd 4	*(SC in next st, INC in next st, SC in next st) from*rep x6 [24]
	From this round work in joining rounds
Rd 5	Ch2, *(DC in next st, 2DC in next st) from*rep x12, sl st in 2nd Ch [37]
Rd 6	Ch2, *(BPdc in next st, 2FPdc in next st) from*rep x18, sl st in 2nd Ch [55]
Rd 7-20	Ch2, *(BPdc in next st, FPdc in next 2sts) from*rep x18, sl st in 2nd Ch [55]
Rd 21	Ch2, *(BPdc in next st, FPdc2tog) from*rep x18, sl st in 2nd Ch [37]
Rd 22	Ch2, DC2tog x18, sl st in 2nd Ch [19]
Rd 23	Ch1, SC in next 18sts, sl st in 1st st of rd [19]
	Cut off thread
	STUFF
	Continue - BLOSSOM END
Rd 24	Green yarn: Ch1, *(SC in next st, SC2tog) from*rep x6, sl st in 1st st of rd [13]
Rd 25	Ch1, SC2tog x6, sl st in 1st st of rd [7]
	Cut off thread leaving a long tail for sewing, pull the tail through edge stitches a tapestry needle, stuff well shaping a cylindrical shape and tighten the opening

STEP 2 STEM.

Green yarn, Work in double strands

	Make an i-cord of 4 stitches about 3cm length or any desired length. Don't cut off thread and continue:
Rd 1	Drop loops 2, 3, 4 off the hook and hold on them. Work a chain stitch into 1st stitch on your hook, then **work SC into a bar between loops, pull the 2nd loop back on your hook and work SC in this loop**. Work this way** to end until no dropped loops left and work last SC into a bar between loops at the end [7]
Rd 2	INC in each of next 7sts [14]
Rd 3	*(SC in next st, INC in next st) from*rep x7 [21]
Rd 4	*(SC in next st, Ch1, DC in next st, Ch1, SC in next 2sts) from*rep x5, sl st in 1st st of rd
	Cut off thread leaving a long tail for sewing
	ASSEMBLE: sew the stem on the pumpkin with a running stitch moving around the stem edge. With this thread pass the needle from the stem to the blossom end "squeezing" the pumpkin shape a bit. Fasten off

WATCH VIDEO TUTORIAL STEM I-CORD AND RD1-3:
https://youtu.be/JtkhqxDI4PA

SCAN ME

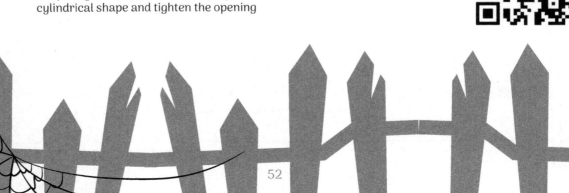

Creepy hat gnome

SIZE: 26 cm / 10 in

	YARN BRAND AND COLORs		TOTAL FOR A PROJECT
Violet	★	Yarn Art Jeans 50	Approx. 25g\90meters
Mustard	★	Yarn Art Jeans 84	Approx. 25g\90meters
Light Green	★	Yarn Art Jeans 29	Approx. 3g\10meters
Black	★	Yarn Art Jeans 53	Just a bit for eyebrows
White	★	Yarn Art Jeans 62	Just a bit for teeth

OTHER MATERIALS	CROCHET STICHES	TOOLS
Stuffing approx. 50g Red colored Safety eyes x2 ø9-10mm	Magic ring, Ch, SC, INC, sl st, SC2tog, FLO, BLO, Bobble st	Crochet hook 2.5 mm

HAT

Use a contrast thread to mark the beginning of each round, do not remove it until the item is completed

HAT (work in continuous rounds)

Rd 1	**Violet:** 6SC in magic ring [6] tighten the ring
Rd 2	SC in each st around [6]
Rd 3	*(SC in next st, INC in next st) from*rep x3 [9]
Rd 4	SC in each st around [9]
Rd 5	*(SC in next st, INC in next st, SC in next st) from*rep x3 [12]
Rd 6-7	SC in each st around [12]
Rd 8	*(SC in next 3sts, INC in next st) from*rep x3 [15]
Rd 9	SC in next 2sts, SC FLO in next 5sts(*), SC in next 8sts [15]
Rd 10	SC in each st around [15]
Rd 11	*(SC in next 2sts, INC in next st, SC in next 2sts) from*rep x3 [18]
Rd 12	SC in next 3sts, SC into next 5sts of prev rd and Rd 8 BLO(*) at the same time(by doing this we gather the hat), SC in next 10sts [18]
Rd 13	SC in each st around [18]
Rd 14	*(SC in next 5sts, INC in next st) from*rep x3 [21]
Rd 15	SC in next 12sts, SC FLO in next 5sts(**), SC in next 4sts [21]
Rd 16	SC in each st around [21]
Rd 17	*(SC in next 3sts, INC in next st, SC in next 3sts) from*rep x3 [24]
Rd 18	SC in next 14sts, SC into next 5sts of prev rd and Rd 14 BLO(**) at the same time(by doing this we gather the hat), SC in next 5sts [24]
Rd 19	SC in each st around [24]
Rd 20	*(SC in next 7sts, INC in next st) from*rep x3 [27]
Rd 21	SC in each st around [27]
Rd 22	SC in next 4sts, SC FLO in next 7sts(***), SC in next 16sts [27]
Rd 23	*(SC in next 4sts, INC in next st, SC in next 4sts) from*rep x3 [30]

Rd 24	SC in each st around [30]
Rd 25	SC in next 5sts, SC into next 7sts of prev rd and Rd 21 BLO(***) at the same time(by doing this we gather the hat), SC in next 18sts [30]
Rd 26	*(SC in next 9sts, INC in next st) from*rep x3 [33]
Rd 27	SC in next 15sts, SC FLO in next 10sts(****), SC in next 8sts [33]
Rd 28	SC in each st around [33]
Rd 29	*(SC in next 5sts, INC in next st, SC in next 5sts) from*rep x3 [36]
Rd 30	SC in next 17sts, SC into next 10sts of prev rd and Rd 26 BLO(****) at the same time, SC in next 9sts [36]
Rd 31	SC in each st around [36]
Rd 32	*(SC in next 11sts, INC in next st) from*rep x3 [39]

Skip 10 stitches from the last stitch to the right and place the first safety eye in between 10th and 11th stitches. Skip 8 more stitches and place the second safety eye in between 8th and 9th stiches. Do not secure them now

Rd 33	SC FLO in each st around [39]
Rd 34	SC in each st around [39]
Rd 35	*(SC in next 6sts, INC in next st, SC in next 6sts) from*rep x3 [42]
Rd 36	*(SC into next 7sts of prev rd and Rd 32 BLO at the same time, SC in next st, SC into next 6sts of prev rd and Rd 32 BLO at the same time) from*rep x3 [42]
Rd 37	SC in each st around [42]
Rd 38	SC FLO in each st around [42]
Rd 39	*(SC in next 3sts, INC in next st, SC in next 3sts) from*rep x6 [48]
Rd 40	SC in each st around [48]
Rd 41	*(SC in next 4sts of prev rd and Rd 37 BLO at the same time, SC in next st, SC in next 3sts of prev rd and Rd 37 BLO at the same time) from*rep x6 [48]
Rd 42	SC in each st around [48]

Continue - HAT BRIM
(work in continuous rounds)

Rd 43	*(SC FLO in next 5sts, INC FLO in next st) from*rep x8 [56]
Rd 44	*(SC in next 3sts, INC in next st, SC in next 3sts) from*rep x8 [64]
Rd 45	*(SC in next 7sts, INC in next st) from*rep x8 [72]
Rd 46	*(SC in next 4sts, INC in next st, SC in next 4sts) from*rep x8 [80]
Rd 47	SC in each st around [80]
Rd 48	sl st in each st around [80]

Cut off thread

Secure the safety eyes, they should be placed in between two gathers (see the last image on page 57)

BODY (work in continuous rounds)

Rd 1-2	Grab a hat upside down, work into stithes BLO of Rd 42 with Mustard: SC BLO in each st around [48]
Rd 3-8	SC in each st around [48]
Rd 10	*(SC in next 7sts, INC in next st) from*rep x6 [54]
Rd 11	*(SC in next 5sts, Bobble st) from*rep x9 [54]
Rd 12	SC in each st around [54]
Rd 13	*(SC in next 2sts, Bobble st, SC in next 3 sts) from*rep x9 [54]
Rd 14	SC in each st around [54]
Rd 15	*(SC in next 5sts, Bobble st) from*rep x9 [54]
Rd 16	SC in each st around [54]
Rd 17	*(SC in next 2sts, Bobble st, SC in next 3sts) from*rep x9 [54]
Rd 18	SC in each st around [54]
Rd 19	*(SC in next 5sts, Bobble st) from*rep x9 [54]
Rd 20	SC in each st around [54]
Rd 21	*(SC in next 2sts, Bobble st, SC in next 3sts) from*rep x9 [54]
Rd 22	SC in each st around [54]
Rd 23	*(SC in next 7sts, SC2tog) from*rep x6 [48]

Rd 24	SC in each st around [48]
Rd 25	SC BLO in each st around [48]
Rd 26	*(SC in next 2sts, SC2tog, SC in next 2sts) from*rep x8 [40]
	Stuff
Rd 27	*(SC in next 3sts, SC2tog) from*rep x8 [32]
Rd 28	*(SC in next st, SC2tog, SC in next st) from*rep x8 [24]
Rd 29	*(SC in next st, SC2tog) from*rep x8 [16]
	Stuff
Rd 30	SC2tog x8 [8]
	Cut off thread. Sew the opening

STEP 4 FACIAL DESIGN

With **Violet** Stitch together two gathers in between the eyes (pic 1)

With **White** color embroider teeth

With **Black** color embroider eyebrows

ARMs (work in continuous rounds)

Rd 1	**Light green:** 5SC in magic ring [5] tighten the ring
Rd 2	INC in each st around [10]
Rd 3-5	SC in each st around [10] Change to Mustard in last st
	Cut off Light Green
Rd 6-7	**Mustard:** SC in each st around [10]
Rd 8	SC BLO in each st around [10]
Rd 9-17	SC in each st around [10]
	Cut off thread leaving a long tail for sewing

NOSE (work in continuous rounds)

	Light green: Foundation chain: Chain 4 [4]
Rd 1	3SC in in 2nd st from hook, SC in next st, 3SC in last st of chain, in other side of a foundation chain: SC in next st [8]
Rd 2	INC in each of next 3sts, SC in next st, INC in each of next 3sts, SC in next st [14]
Rd 3-4	SC in each st around [14]
	Cut off thread leaving a long tail for sewing. Stuff the nose a bit

BOOTS x2 (work in continuous rounds)

Rd 1	**Mustard:** 6SC in magic ring [6] tighten the ring
Rd 2	INC in each st around [12]
Rd 3	*(SC in next st, INC in next st) from*rep x6 [18]
Rd 4-6	SC in each st around [18]
Rd 7	*(SC in next st, SC2tog) from*rep x6 [12]
	Stuff. Close an opening by stitch edges together with SC across
	Cut off thread leaving a long tail for sewing.

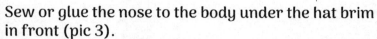

Sew or glue the nose to the body under the hat brim in front (pic 3).
Sew the arms on the body on sides under the hat brim (pic 4)
Attach the boots to Rd 24 FLO of the body (pic 1-2)

Fall Gnome

SIZE: 26 cm / 10 in

YARN BRAND AND COLORs			TOTAL FOR A PROJECT
Brown	★	Yarn Art Jeans 40	Approx. 40g/140 meters
Wheat	★	Yarn Art Jeans 05	Approx. 12g/40 meters
Honey caramel	★	Yarn Art Jeans 07	Approx. 10g/35 meters
Dark Green	★	Yarn Art Jeans 82	Approx. 2 g
Bright Yellow	★	Yarn Art Jeans 35	Approx. 2 g
Mustard	★	Yarn Art Jeans 84	Approx. 2 g
Pumpkin Orange	★	Yarn Art Jeans 85	Approx. 1 g

OTHER MATERIALS	CROCHET STICHES	TOOLS
Stuffing approx. 50g Yellow beads ø7 mm x3 Yellow bead ø20 mm x1 Red beads ø10 mm x3	Magic ring, Ch, SC, INC, DC, hdc, sl st, SC2tog, FLO, BLO	Crochet hook 2.5 mm

HAT+BODY

Use a contrast thread to mark the beginning of each round, do not remove it until the item is completed

STEP 1 HAT (work in continuous rounds)

Rd 1	**Brown:** 6SC in magic ring [6] tighten the ring
Rd 2	SC in each st around [6]
Rd 3	*(SC in next st, INC in next st) from*rep x3 [9]
Rd 4	SC in each st around [9]
Rd 5	*(SC in next st, INC in next st, SC in next st) from*rep x3 [12]
Rd 6	SC in each st around [12]
Rd 7	*(SC in next st, INC in next st, SC in next st) from*rep x4 [16]
Rd 8-9	SC in each st around [16]
Rd 10	*(SC in next 3sts, INC in next st) from*rep x4 [20]
Rd 11-12	SC in each st around [20]
Rd 13	*(SC in next 2sts, INC in next st, SC in next 2sts) from*rep x4 [24]
Rd 14-15	SC in each st around [24]
Rd 16	*(SC in next 5sts, INC in next st) from*rep x4 [28]
Rd 17-18	SC in each st around [28]
Rd 19	*(SC in next 3sts, INC in next st, SC in next 3sts) from*rep x4 [32]
Rd 20-21	SC in each st around [32]
Rd 22	*(SC in next 7sts, INC in next st) from*rep x4 [36]
Rd 23-24	SC in each st around [36]
Rd 25	*(SC in next 4sts, INC in next st, SC in next 4sts) from*rep x4 [40]
Rd 26-27	SC in each st around [40]
Rd 28	*(SC in next 9sts, INC in next st) from*rep x4 [44]
Rd 29-30	SC in each st around [44]
Rd 31	*(SC in next 5sts, INC in next st, SC in next 5sts) from*rep x4 [48]
Rd 32-33	SC in each st around [48]
Rd 34	*(SC in next 11sts, INC in next st) from*rep x4 [52]

Rd 35-36	SC in each st around [52]
Rd 37	*(SC in next 6sts, INC in next st, SC in next 6sts) from*rep x4 [56]
Rd 38	SC in each st around [56]
Rd 39	SC BLO in each st around [56]
Rd 40	SC in next 12sts, SC BLO in next 4sts(we will attach the arm to these sts), SC in next 8sts, SC BLO in next 8sts(we will attach the beard to these sts), SC in next 8sts, SC BLO in next 4sts(we will attach the arm to these sts), SC in next 12sts [56]
Rd 41-45	SC in each st around [56]
Rd 46	*(SC in next 13sts, INC in next st) from*rep x4 [60]
Rd 47-50	SC in each st around [60]
Rd 51	*(SC in next 7sts, INC in next st, SC in next 7sts) from*rep x4 [64]
Rd 52-53	SC in each st around [64]
Rd 54	*(SC in next 3sts, SC2tog, SC in next 3sts) from*rep x8 [56]
Rd 55-57	SC in each st around [56]
Rd 58	*(SC in next 5sts, SC2tog) from*rep x8 [48]
	Stuff
Rd 59-60	SC in each st around [48]
Rd 61	SC BLO in each st around [48]
Rd 62	*(SC in next 2sts, SC2tog, SC in next 2sts) from*rep x8 [40]
Rd 63	*(SC in next 3sts, SC2tog) from*rep x8 [32]
Rd 64	*(SC in next st, SC2tog, SC in next st) from*rep x8 [24]
Rd 65	*(SC in next st, SC2tog) from*rep x8 [16]
	Stuff
Rd 66	SC2tog x8 [8] Cut off thread and sew the opening

STEP 2 STAND

Rd 1	With a new **Brown** work into stitch FLO of Rd 60 of the body: Ch1, SC FLO in each st around [48]

Cut off thread

STEP 3 HAT BRIM (work in continuous rounds)

Rd 1	Grab the body upside-down. With a new **Brown** work into stitches FLO of Rd 38 of the hat: *(SC FLO in next 13sts, INC FLO in next st) from*rep x4 [60]
Rd 2	*(SC in next 7sts, INC next st, SC in next 7sts) from*rep x4 [64]
Rd 3	*(SC in next 15sts, INC in next st) from rep x4 [68]
Rd 4	*(SC in next 8sts, INC next st, SC in next 8sts) from*rep x4 [72]
Rd 5	sl st in each st around [72]

Cut off thread

ARMs (work in continuous rounds)

Rd 1	**Honey Caramel:** 5SC in magic ring [5] tighten the ring
Rd 2	INC in each st around [10]
Rd 3-5	SC in each st around [10] Change to Brown in last st

Cut off Honey caramel

Rd 6-7	**Brown:** SC in each st around [10]
Rd 8	SC BLO in each st around [10]
Rd 9-17	SC in each st around[10]

Cut off thread leaving a long tail for sewing

NOSE (work in continuous rounds)

Rd 1	**Honey Caramel:** 6SC in magic ring [6] tighten the ring
Rd 2	INC in each st around [12]
Rd 3	*(SC in next st, INC in next st) from*rep x6 [18]
Rd 4-5	SC in each st around [18]
Rd 6	*(SC in next st, SC2tog) from*rep x6 [12]

Cut off thread leaving a long tail for sewing. Stuff the nose a bit

BEARD (work in continuous rounds)

Rd 1	**Wheat:** SC4 in magic ring [4] tighten the ring
Rd 2	*(SC in next st, INC in next st) from*rep x2 [6]
Rd 3	INC in each of next 2sts, SC in next 2sts, INC in next st, SC in next st [9]
Rd 4	SC in next st, INC in each of next 2sts, SC in next 5sts, INC in next st [12]
Rd 5	SC in next 2sts, INC in each of next 2sts, SC in next 5sts, INC in next st, SC in next 2sts [15]
Rd 6	SC in next 3sts, INC in each of next 2sts, SC in next 9sts, INC in next st [18]
Rd 7	SC in next 4sts, INC in each of next 2sts, SC in next 8sts, INC in next st, SC in next 3sts [21]
Rd 8	SC in next 5sts, INC in each of next 2sts, SC in next 14sts [23]
Rd 9	SC in next 6sts, INC in each of next 2sts, SC in next 14sts, INC in next st [26]
Rd 10-12	SC in each st around [26]
Rd 13	SC in next 8sts, SC2tog, SC in next 11sts, SC2tog, SC in next 3sts [24]
Rd 14	SC in next 7sts, SC2tog, SC in next 10sts, SC2tog, SC in next 3sts [22]
Rd 15-17	SC in each st around [22]

Cut off thread leaving a long tail for sewing. Sew or glue the nose o the beard

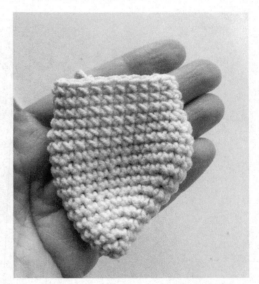

LEAF (make in different colors)

Foundation chain: Chain 8

Rd 1

Sl st in 2nd st from hook, sl st in next 6sts, Ch 1,

In other side of the foundation chain: SC in next st,

hdc in next st,

2DC in each of next 2sts,

hdc in next st,

SC in next st,

sl st in next st,

Ch 2,

Turn

Sl st in 2nd st from hook,

Row 2

SC BLO in next st ,

hdc BLO in next st,

DC BLO in next 2sts, hdc BLO in next st,

SC BLO in next st,

sl st BLO in next st,

Cut off thread

OVAL LEAF (use different colors)

Foundation chain: Chain 5 [5]

Rd 1 Sl st in 2nd st from hook, SC in next st, hdc in next st, 6DC in next st (a last stitch of chain), in other side of a foundation chain: hdc in next st, SC in next st, sl st in next st [12]

Cut off thread

Sew the beard with the nose to the body under the hat brim in front (8 stitches FLO made in Rd 39 of the body).
Sew the arms on the body on sides (4 stitches FLO for each arm made in Rd 39 of the body)

Candy corn Gnome

SIZE: 26 cm / 10 in

YARN BRAND AND COLORs			TOTAL FOR A PROJECT
Pumpkin Orange	★	Yarn Art Jeans 85	Approx. 25 g/80 meters
Bright Yellow	★	Yarn Art Jeans 35	Approx. 12 g/40 meters
Wheat	★	Yarn Art Jeans 05	Approx. 5 g/20 meters
White	★	Yarn Art Jeans 62	Approx. 10 g/35 meters

OTHER MATERIALS	CROCHET STICHES	TOOLS
Stuffing approx. 60g	Magic ring, Ch, SC, INC, sl st, SC2tog, FLO, BLO	Crochet hook 2.5 mm

HAT+BODY

Use a contrast thread to mark the beginning of each round. Do not remove it until your work is completed

STEP 1 HAT (work in continuous rounds)

Rd 1	**White:** 6SC in magic ring [6] tighten the ring
Rd 2	INC in in each st around [12]
Rd 3	SC in each st around [12]
Rd 4	*(SC in next st, INC in next st, SC in next st) from*rep x4 [16]
Rd 5-6	SC in each st around[16]
Rd 7	*(SC in next 3sts, INC in next st) from*rep x4 [20]
Rd 8-9	SC in each st around [20]
Rd 10	*(SC in next 2sts, INC in next st, SC in next 2sts) from*rep x4 [24]
Rd 11-12	SC in each st around [24]
Rd 13	*(SC in next 5sts, INC in next st) from*rep x4 [28]
Rd 14-15	SC in each st around [28]
Rd 16	*(SC in next 3sts, INC in next st, SC in next 3sts) from*rep x4 [32]
Rd 17-18	SC in each st around[32] Change to Bright yellow in last st. Cut off White
Rd 19	**Bright yellow:** *(SC in next 7sts, INC in next st) from*rep x4 [36]
Rd 20-21	SC in each st around [36]
Rd 22	*(SC in next 4sts, INC in next st, SC in next 4sts) from*rep x4 [40]
Rd 23-24	SC in each st around [40]
Rd 25	*(SC in next 9sts, INC in next st) from*rep x4 [44]
Rd 26-27	SC in each st around [44]
Rd 28	*(SC in next 5sts, INC in next st, SC in next 5sts) from*rep x4 [48]
Rd 29-30	SC in each st around[48]
Rd 31	*(SC in next 11sts, INC in next st) from*rep x4 [52]
Rd 32-33	SC in each st around [52]
Rd 34	*(SC in next 6sts, INC in next st, SC in next 6sts) from*rep x4 [56]

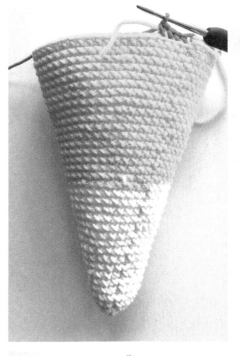

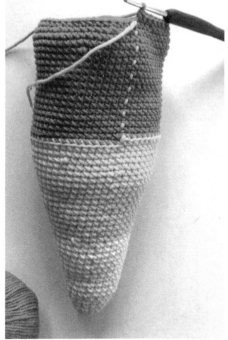

Rd 35-36	SC in each st around [56] Change to Pumpkin orange in last st. Cut off Bright yellow
Rd 37	**Pumpkin Orange:** SC BLO in each st around [56]
Rd 38	SC in next 11sts, SC BLO in next 5sts (we will attach the arm to these sts), SC in next 8sts, SC BLO in next 8sts (we will attach a nose to these sts), SC in next 8sts, SC BLO in next 5sts (we will attach the arm to these sts), SC in next 11sts [56]
Rd 39-45	SC in each st around [56]
Rd 46	*(SC in next 13sts, INC in next st) from*rep x4 [60]
Rd 47-50	SC in each st around [60]
Rd 51	*(SC in next 7sts, INC in next st, SC in next 7sts) from*rep x4 [64]
Rd 52-53	SC in each st around [64]
Rd 54	*(SC in next 3sts, SC2tog, SC in next 3sts) from*rep x8[56]
Rd 55-57	SC in each st around [56]
	Stuff
Rd 58	*(SC in next 5sts, SC2tog) from*rep x8 [48]
Rd 59	SC in each st around [48]
Rd 60	SC BLO in each st around [48]
Rd 61	*(SC in next 2sts, SC2tog, SC in next 2sts) from*rep x8[40]
	Stuff
Rd 62	*(SC in next 3sts, SC2tog) from*rep x8[32]
Rd 63	*(SC in next st, SC2tog, SC in next st) from*rep x8 [24]
Rd 64	*(SC in next st, SC2tog) from*rep x8 [16]
	Stuff
Rd 65	SC2tog x8 [8]

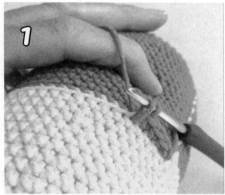

Cut off thread and sew the opening

STEP 2 HAT BRIM (work in continuous rounds)

Rd 1	Grab the body upside-down, with **Pumpkin Orange:** work in stitches FLO of Rd 36 of the body :*(SC FLO in next 13sts, INC FLO in next st) from*rep x4 [60] (pic 1)
Rd 2	*(SC in next 7sts, INC in next st, SC in next 7sts) from*rep x4 [64]
Rd 3	*(SC in next 15sts, INC in next st) from*rep x4 [68]
Rd 4	*(SC in next 8sts, INC in next st, SC in next 8sts) from*rep x4 [72]

Cut off thread

BEARD (work in continuous rounds)

Rd 1	**White:** 6SC in magic ring [6] tighten the ring
Rd 2	INC in in each st around [12]
Rd 3	SC in each st around [12]
Rd 4	*(SC in next st, INC in next st) from*rep x6[18]
Rd 5	SC in each st around [18]
Rd 6	*(SC in next st, INC in next st, SC in next st) from*rep x6 [24]
Rd 7	SC in each st around [24]
Rd 8	*(SC in next 7sts, INC in next st) from*rep x3 [27]
Rd 9-11	SC in each st around [27]
Rd 12	*(SC in next 7sts, SC2tog) from*rep x3 [24]
Rd 13	*(SC in next 3sts, SC2tog, SC in next 3sts) from*rep x3 [21]

NOSE (work in continuous rounds)

Rd 1	**Wheat:** 6SC in magic ring [6] tighten the ring
Rd 2	INC in each st around [12]
Rd 3	*(SC in next st, INC in next st) from*rep x6 [18]
Rd 4-5	SC in each st around [18]
Rd 6	*(SC in next st, SC2tog) from*rep x6 [12]
	Cut off thread leaving a long tail for sewing. Stuff a bit
	Sew or glue the nose on the beard

ARMs (work in continuous rounds)

STEP 1 ARM

Rd 1	**Wheat:** 5SC in magic ring [5] tighten the ring
Rd 2	INC in each st around [10]
Rd 3-5	SC in each st around [10] Change to Pumpkin orange in last st. Cut off thread
Rd 6-7	**Pumpkin Orange:** SC in each st around [10]
Rd 8	SC BLO in each st around [10]
Rd 9-17	SC in each st around [10]
	Cut off thread leaving a long tail for sewing

STEP 2 CUFF

Rd 1	**Pumpkin Orange:** SC FLO in stitches in stithes of Rd 7 [10]
Rd 2	SC in each st around [10]
	Cut off thread

Sew or glue the nose with the beard to the body under the hat brim in front (8 stitches FLO).
Sew the arms on the body on sides (4 stitches FLO for each arm)

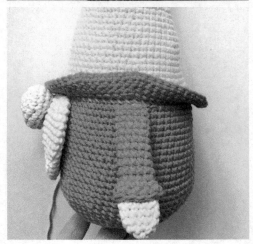

Creepy clown

SIZE: 26 cm / 10 in

YARN BRAND AND COLORs			TOTAL FOR A PROJECT
Fog Gray	★	Yarn Art Jeans 49	Approx. 20g/70meters
White	★	Yarn Art Jeans 62	Approx. 10g/30meters
Red	★	Yarn Art Jeans 90	Approx. 10g/30meters
Black	★	Yarn Art Jeans 53	Approx. 2g
Bright Yellow	★	Yarn Art Jeans 35	Approx. 1g
Pumpkin Orange	★	Yarn Art Jeans 85	Approx. 10g/30meters

Red colored
Safety eyes

OTHER MATERIALS	CROCHET STICHES	TOOLS
Stuffing approx. 60g Red colored Safety eyes x2 ø9-10mm Thin Wooden craft dowel x1	Magic ring, Ch, SC, hdc, DC, INC, sl st, SC2tog, FLO, BLO	Crochet hook 2.5 mm, 2 mm (for eyes)

HAT+BODY

Note: Use a contrast thread to mark the beginning of each round

STEP 1 HAT (work in continuous rounds)

Rd 1	**Fog gray:** 6SC in magic ring [6] tighten the ring
Rd 2	SC in each st around [6]
Rd 3	*(SC in next st, INC in next st) from*rep x3[9]
Rd 4	SC in each st around [9]
Rd 5	*(SC in next st, INC in next st, SC in next st) from*rep x3 [12]
Rd 6	SC in each st around [12]
Rd 7	*(SC in next st, INC in next st, SC in next st) from*rep x4 [16]
Rd 8-9	SC in each st around [16]
Rd 10	*(SC in next 3sts, INC in next st) from*rep x4 [20]
Rd 11-12	SC in each st around [20]
Rd 13	*(SC in next 2sts, INC in next st, SC in next 2sts) from*rep x4 [24]
Rd 14-15	SC in each st around [24]
Rd 16	*(SC in next 5sts, INC in next st) from*rep x4 [28]
Rd 17-18	SC in each st around [28]
Rd 19	*(SC in next 3sts, INC in next st, SC in next 3sts) from*rep x4 [32]
Rd 20-21	SC in each st around [32]
Rd 22	*(SC in next 7sts, INC in next st) from*rep x4 [36]
Rd 23-24	SC in each st around [36]
Rd 25	*(SC in next 4sts, INC in next st, SC in next 4sts) from*rep x4 [40]
Rd 26-27	SC in each st around [40]
Rd 28	*(SC in next 9sts, INC in next st) from*rep x4 [44]
Rd 29-30	SC in each st around [44]
Rd 31	*(SC in next 5sts, INC in next st, SC in next 5sts) from*rep x4 [48]
Rd 32-33	SC in each st around [48]
Rd 34-36	SC BLO in each st around [48]
Rd 37-40	SC in each st around [48]

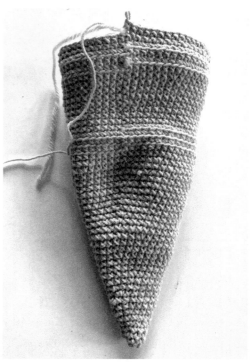

Rd 41	*(SC in next 11sts, INC in next st) from*rep x4[52]
Rd 42-43	SC in each st around [52]
Rd 44	*(SC in next 6sts, INC in next st, SC in next 6sts) from*rep x4 [56]
Rd 45	SC in each st around [56]
Rd 46	SC BLO in each st around [56]
Rd 47	SC in each st around [56]
Rd 48	SC BLO in each st around [56]
Rd 49	*(SC in next 13sts, INC in next st) from*rep x4 [60]
	Drop a loop from a hook

With a new **Fog gray:** Surface slip stitches into Rd 46 around [56]
Cut off thread
With a new **Fog gray:** Surface slip stitches into Rd 47 around [56]
Cut off thread

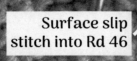

Surface slip stitch into Rd 46

Here we work Surface slip stitch into Rd 47

Rd 50-52	Grab the dropped loop and continue SC in each st around [60]
Rd 53	*(SC in next 13sts, SC2tog) from*rep x4 [56]
Rd 54	SC in each st around [56]
Rd 55	*(SC in next 5sts, SC2tog) from*rep x8 [48]
Rd 56	SC in each st around [48]
Rd 57	SC BLO in each st around [48]
Rd 58	*(SC in next 2sts, SC2tog, SC in next 2sts) from*rep x8 [40]
	Stuff
Rd 59	*(SC in next 3sts, SC2tog) from*rep x8 [32]
Rd 60	*(SC in next st, SC2tog, SC in next st) from*rep x8 [24]
Rd 61	*(SC in next st, SC2tog) from*rep x8 [16]
	Stuff
Rd 62	SC2tog x8 [8]
	Cut off thread and sew the opening

STEP 2 SKIRT

| Rd 1 | Hold the body upside-down. With a new **Fog gray** work into stitches FLO of Rd 47: *(hdc FLO in next 6sts, 2hdc FLO in next st) from*rep x8 [64]

Cut off thread |

STEP 3 COLLAR

| Rd 1 | **White:** work in stitches FLO of Rd 34: 4DC FLO in each st around

Cut off thread |

STEP 4 NOSE (work in continuous rounds)

	Red: Foundation chain: Chain 4 [4]
Rd 1	3SC in 2nd st from hook, SC in next st, 3SC in last st of foundation chain, in bottom of chain: SC in next st [8]
Rd 2	INC in each next 3sts, SC in next st, INC in each of next 3sts, SC in next st [14]
Rd 3-4	SC in each st around [14]

Cut off thread leaving a long tail for sewing. Stuff the nose

ARMs (work in continuous rounds)

STEP 1 PALMS

Rd 1	**White:** 5SC in magic ring [5] tighten the ring
Rd 2	INC in each st around [10]
Rd 3-5	SC in each st around [10] Change to Fog gray in last st.
	Cut off White
Rd 6-7	**Fog gray:** SC in each st around [10]
Rd 8	SC BLO in each st around [10]
Rd 9-17	SC in each st around [10]

Cut off thread leaving a long tail for sewing

STEP 2 CUFF

Rd 1	With new **Fog gray** work into stitches FLO of Rd 7: *(hdc FLO in next st, 2hdc FLO in next st) from*rep to end [15]

Cut off thread

BOOTS (work in continuous rounds)

STEP 1 BOOT

Rd 1	**Fog gray:** 6SC in magic ring [6] tighten the ring
Rd 2	INC in each st around [12]
Rd 3	*(SC in next st, INC in next st) from*rep x6 [18]
Rd 4-6	SC in each st around [18]
Rd 7	*(SC in next st, SC2tog) from*rep x6 [12]

Cut off thread leaving a long tail for sewing. Stitch opening flat by SC across and attach legs to Rd 56 of the body

STEP 2 POMPON

Rd 1	**Red:** 5SC in magic ring [5] tighten the ring
Rd 2	INC in each st around [10]
Rd 3-4	SC in each st around [10]

Cut off leaving a long tail. Pull the thread through stitches of the last round and tighten. Sew to the boot

HAIR (make x2, on the sides)   (work in continuous rounds)

	Pumpkin orange: Chain 2 [2]
Rd 1	3SC in 2nd st from hook [3]
Rd 2	INC in each of next 3SC [6]
Rd 3	INC in each of next 2sts, SC in next 2sts, INC in next st, SC in next st [9]
Rd 4	SC in next st, INC in each of next 2sts, SC in next 5sts, INC in next st [12]
Rd 5	SC in next 2sts, INC in each of next 2sts, SC in next 5sts, INC in next st, SC in next 2sts [15]
Rd 6	SC in next 3sts, INC in each of next 2sts, SC in next 9sts, INC in next st [18]
Rd 7	SC in next 14sts, SC2tog, SC in next 2sts [17]
Rd 8	SC in next 4sts, SC2tog, SC in next 7sts, SC2tog, SC in next 2sts [15]
Rd 9	SC in next 4sts, SC2tog, SC in next 6sts, SC2tog, SC in next st [13]

Cut off thread leaving a long tail for sewing

HAIR (on top)   (work in continuous rounds)

	Pumpkin orange: Chain 2 [2]
Rd 1	3SC in 2nd st from hook [3] (work in round)
Rd 2	INC in each of next 3SC [6]
Rd 3	INC in each of next 2sts, SC in next 2sts, INC in next st, SC in next st [9]
Rd 4	SC in next st, INC in each of next 2sts, SC in next 5sts, INC in next st [12]
Rd 5	SC in next 2sts, INC in each of next 2sts, SC in next 5sts, INC in next st, SC in next 2sts [15]
Rd 6	SC in next 3sts, INC in each of next 2sts, SC in next 9sts, INC in next st [18]
Rd 7	SC in next 4sts, INC in each of next 2sts, SC in next 8sts, INC in next st, SC in next 3sts [21]
Rd 8	SC in next 4sts, SC2tog, SC in next 9sts, SC2tog, SC in next 4sts [19]
Rd 9	SC in next 4sts, SC2tog, SC in next 8sts, SC2tog, SC in next 3sts [17]

Cut off thread leaving a long tail for sewing

EYES. Crochet Hook 2mm

Each eye consists of 2 crocheted parts:
1. Sclera – Bright yellow
2. Upper eyelid – Fog gray
As well I use colored safety eyes

STEP 1 SCLERA (make x2)

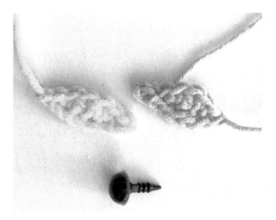

	Bright Yellow: Foundation chain: Chain 7 [7]
Row 1	sl st in 2nd st from hook, SC in next st, hdc in next 2sts, SC in next st, sl st in next st [6]
	Cut off thread
	Insert a safety eye in between two hdc and secure it

STEP 2 UPPER EYELID (make x2)

	Fog gray: Foundation chain: Chain 6 [6]
Rd 1	Work around the foundation chain: sl st in 2nd st from hook, SC in next st, DC in next st, SC in next st, sl st in next st, Ch2, sl st in 2nd st from hook, sl st in next 5sts
	Cut off thread leaving a long tail for sewing

STEP 3 ASSEMBLE

Insert the tail of Fog gray thread through the eye of the tapestry needle. **Arrange parts** as it's illustrated in image (the upper eyelid covers the safety eye) **and stitch edges of the yellow and gray parts together.**

Sew or glue the nose to the hat right above the collar in front of the body **and then attach (sew or glue) eyes.**

Attach the arms to the body under the collar on sides.

SMILE

STEP 1 BLACK PART OF A MOUTH

	Black: Foundation chain: Chain 7 [7]
Row 1	SC in 2nd st from hook, SC in next 5sts [6] Turn
Row 2	Ch1, SC2tog, SC in next 2sts, SC2tog [4] Turn
Row 3	Ch1, SC in next st, SC2tog, SC in next st [3] Turn
Row 4	Ch1, SC2tog, SC in next st [2]
	Cut off thread

STEP 2 TEETH

	White: Chain 5 [5]
Row 1	SC in 2nd st from hook, SC in next 3sts, Ch5, SC in 2nd ch from hook, SC in next 3sts of Ch5.
	Cut off thread

STEP 3 JOINING ALL PARTS TOGETHER

Red: Chain 30, then join the black part (step 1) and work around the edge: Joining: slip st into Ch1 of the foundation chain.
1. Then work into side edge stitches: sl st into each of 4 rows across the edge.
2. Then work 2SC into each of next 2 SC of Row 4;
3. Then continue working on the other side: sl st into each of 4 rows across the edge.
4. Chain 30

Cut off thread leaving a long tail for sewing

With a new Red: stitch teeth to the black part with slip stitches working across the top edge inserting the hook through all items

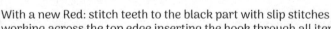

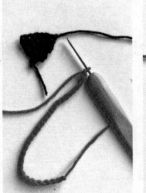 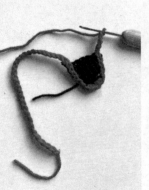  

STEP 4 ASSEMBLE

First, pin the mouth to place under the collar and the nose in front. Using Red thread and tapestry needle sew the mouth to the gnome. As well you can glue it.

Sew or glue hair to sides right above the collar and one on the top of the hat

Attach hair to the head (on the top and on sides)

BALL (work in continuous rounds)

Rd 1	**Red:** 6SC in magic ring [6] tighten the ring
Rd 2	INC in each st around [12]
Rd 3	*(SC in next st, INC in next st) from*rep x6 [18]
Rd 4	*(SC in next st, INC in next st, SC in next st) from*rep x6 [24]
Rd 5	SC in each st around [24]
Rd 6	*(SC in next 3sts, INC in next st) from*rep x6 [30]
Rd 7-15	SC in each st around [30]
Rd 16	*(SC in next 3sts, SC2tog) from*rep x6 [24]
Rd 17	SC in each st around [24]
Rd 18	*(SC in next st, SC2tog, SC in next st) from*rep x6 [18]
Rd 19	*(SC in next st, SC2tog) from*rep x6 [12]
	Stuff well
Rd 20	*(SC in next st, SC2tog) from*rep x4 [8]
Rd 21	2hdc FLO in each st around [16]

Cut off thread

Insert the wooden craft dowel into the opening and tighten with a thread

As well you can use some glue to secure the stick into place

Embroider using a white thread "You'll float too"

91

Cookies without a
crocheted eye

Cookies with a
crocheted eye and a
safety eye inside

Spooky cookies

USE ANY COLORS YOU LIKE TO MAKE THESE CUTE SPOOKY COOKIES

	YARN BRAND AND COLORs	TOTAL FOR A PROJECT
Black ★	Yarn Art Jeans 28	Approx. 3 g
Bright Yellow ★	Yarn Art Jeans 35	Approx. 3 g
Pumpkin Orange ★	Yarn Art Jeans 85	Approx. 3 g
Violet ★	Yarn Art Jeans 50	Approx. 3 g
White ★	Yarn Art Jeans 62	Approx. 3 g
Light Blue ★	Yarn Art Jeans 75	Approx. 1 g

OTHER MATERIALS	CROCHET STICHES	TOOLS
Stuffing approx. 3g for 1 cookie Optional: black safety eyes 13-15mm Wiggle EYES Glue	Magic ring, Ch, SC, INC, sl st, SC2tog, FLO, BLO, FPsc, FP/BP, FPSC2_tog	Crochet hook 2.5 mm

If you are going to crochet cookies without crocheted eye, follow the pattern using one color without color changing

Rd 1	**Black color:** 6SC in magic ring [6] tighten the ring
Rd 2	INC in each st around [12]
Rd 3	**Color for an iris:** *(SC in next st, INC in next st) from*rep x6 [18]
Rd 4	**White color:** *(SC in next st, INC in next st, SC in next st) from*rep x6 [24]

If you are going to use a safety eye, place it and secure

Rd 5	*(SC BLO in next 3sts, INC BLO in next st) from*rep x6 [30]
Rd 6	*(SC in next 4sts, FPsc in next st) from*rep x6 [30]
Rd 7	*(SC in next 3sts, INC in next st, FPsc in FPsc of prev row) from*rep x6 [36]
Rd 8	*(SC in next 5sts, FPsc in FPsc of prev row) from*rep x6 [36]
Rd 9	*(SC in next 4sts, FPsc in FPsc of prev row) from*rep x6 [30]
Rd 10	*(SC in next 3sts, FPsc in FPsc of prev row) from*rep x6 [24]
Rd 11	*(SC in next 2sts, FPsc in FPsc of prev row) from*rep x6 [18]
Rd 12	*(SC in next st, FPsc in FPsc of prev row) from*rep x6 [12]
Rd 13	FPsc in each of FPsc of prev row around [6]
Rd 14	FPsc in next 6sts [6]
Rd 15	FPSC2_tog x3, Ch1 [3]

Cut off thread, pull it throught ch

Glue wiggle eyes and embroider smiles

Slimy Candy Corn

SIZE: 26 cm / 10 in

YARN BRAND AND COLORs			TOTAL FOR A PROJECT
Light Green	☆	YarnArt Jeans 76	Approx. 7 g/20 meters
Black	★	YarnArt Jeans 28	Approx. 20 g/70 meters
Honey Caramel	☆	YarnArt Jeans 07	Approx. 5 g/15 meters
White	☆	YarnArt Jeans 62	Approx. 10 g/35 meters
Bright Yellow	☆	YarnArt Jeans 35	Approx. 10 g/35 meters
Pumpkin Orange	★	YarnArt Jeans 85	Approx. 10 g/35 meters
Violet (for a cord)	★	Yarn Art Jeans 50	Approx. 1 g

OTHER MATERIALS	CROCHET STICHES	TOOLS
Stuffing approx. 40g	Magic ring, Ch, SC, hdc, INC, sl st, SC2tog, FLO, BLO	Crochet hook 2.5 mm

HAT

Use a contrast thread to mark the beginning of each round. Do not remove it until your work is completed

STEP 1 GREEN SLIME (work in continuous rounds)

Rd 1	**Light Green:** 6SC in magic ring [6] tighten the ring
Rd 2	*(INC in next st, SC in next st) from*rep x3 [9]
Rd 3-4	SC in each st around [9]
Rd 5	*(SC in next sts, INC in next st, SC in next st) from*rep x3 [12]
Rd 6-7	SC in each st around [12]
Rd 8	*(INC in next st, SC in next 3sts) from*rep x3 [15]
Rd 9-10	SC in each st around [15]
Rd 11	*(SC in next 2sts, INC in next st, SC in next 2sts) from*rep x3 [18]
Rd 12-13	SC in each st around [18]
Rd 14	*(INC in next st, SC in next 5sts) from*rep x3 [21]
Rd 15-16	SC in each st around [21]
Rd 17	Make drips, 1st drip: Chain 6 (pic.1),
	hdc in 2nd Ch from hook (pic.2),
	hdc in each st of chain (pic.3),
	hdc in stitch of main part where Ch6 comes from (pic.4),
	skip next st of a main part, SC FLO in next 2sts of main part(pic.5)
	2nd Drip: Chain 5, hdc in 2nd Ch from hook, hdc in each st of chain, hdc in stitch of main part where Ch5 comes from, skip next st of a main part, SC FLO in next st of main part,

4

5

3rd Drip: Chain 4, hdc in 2nd Ch from hook, hdc in each st of chain, hdc in stitch of main part where Ch4 comes from, skip next st of a main part, SC FLO in next st of main part,

4th Drip: Chain 4, hdc in 2nd Ch from hook, hdc in each st of chain, hdc in stitch of main part where Ch4 comes from, skip next st of a main part, SC FLO in next 2sts of main part

5th Drip: Chain 3, hdc in 2nd Ch from hook, hdc in each st of chain, hdc in stitch of main part where Ch3 comes from, skip next st of a main part, SC FLO in next 2sts of main part,

6th Drip: Chain 5, hdc in 2nd Ch from hook, hdc in each st of chain, hdc in stitch of main part where Ch5 comes from, skip next st of a main part, SC FLO in next st of main part, sl st FLO in next st of a main part.
Cut of Light green

STEP 2 BLACK PART of the hat (work in continuous rounds)

Rd 1	Start from the last stitch of Rd 16 of Step 1 Green Slime, with **Black:** SC BLO in each st around [21]
Rd 2	*(SC in next 3sts, INC in next st, SC in next 3sts) from*rep x3 [24]
Rd 3	SC in each st around [24]
Rd 4	*(SC in next 7sts, INC in next st) from*rep x3 [27]
Rd 5	SC in each st around [27]
Rd 6	*(SC in next 4sts, INC in next st, SC in next 4sts) from*rep x3 [30]
Rd 7	SC in each st around [30]
Rd 8	*(SC in next 9sts, INC in next st) from*rep x3 [33]
Rd 9	SC in each st around [33]
Rd 10	*(SC in next 5sts, INC in next st, SC in next 5sts) from*rep x3 [36]
Rd 11	SC in each st around [36]
Rd 12	*(SC in next 11sts, INC in next st) from*rep x3 [39]
Rd 13	SC in each st around [39]
Rd 14	*(SC in next 6sts, INC in next st, SC in next 6sts) from*rep x3 [42]
Rd 15-16	SC in each st around [42]
Rd 17	*(SC in next 13sts, INC in next st) from*rep x3 [45]
Rd 18-19	SC in each st around [45]
Rd 20	*(SC in next 7sts, INC in next st, SC in next 7sts) from*rep x3 [48]

STEP 3 CONTINUE - HAT BRIM

Rd 21	SC FLO in each st around [48]
Rd 22	*(SC in next 5sts, INC in next st) from*rep x8 [56]
Rd 23	*(SC in next 3sts, INC in next st, SC in next 3sts) from*rep x8 [64]
Rd 24	*(SC in next 3sts, INC in next st) from*rep x16 [80]
Rd 25	*(SC in next 2sts, INC in next st, SC in next 2sts) from*rep x16 [96]
	Cut off Black

BODY (work in continuous rounds)

Rd 1	Hold the head upside-down, with **White** work in stitches BLO of Rd 20 Step 2: SC BLO in each st around [48]
Rd 2	SC in next 10sts, SC BLO in next 4sts (we will attach the arm to these sts), SC in next 8sts, SC BLO in next 4sts (we will attach mustache to these sts), SC in next 8sts, SC BLO in next 4sts (we will attach the arm to these sts), SC in next 10sts [48]
Rd 3-4	SC in each st around [48]
Rd 5	*(SC in next 11sts, INC in next st) from*rep x4 [52]
Rd 6-7	SC in each st around [52] Change to Bright Yellow in last st. Cut off White
Rd 8	**Bright Yellow:** *(SC in next 6sts, INC in next st, SC in next 6sts) from*rep x4 [56]
Rd 9-10	SC in each st around [56]
Rd 11	*(SC in next 13sts, INC in next st) from*rep x4 [60]
Rd 12	SC in each st around [60]
Rd 13	*(SC in next 7sts, INC in next st, SC in next 7sts) from*rep x4 [64]
Rd 14	SC in each st around [64] Change to Pumpkin Orange. Cut off Bright yellow
Rd 15	**Pumpkin Orange:** SC in each st around [64]
Rd 16	*(SC in next 3sts, SC2tog, SC in next 3sts) from*rep x8 [56]
Rd 17-18	SC in each st around [56]
Rd 19	*(SC in next 5sts, SC2tog) from*rep x8 [48]
	Stuff
Rd 20-21	SC in each st around [48]
Rd 22	SC BLO in each st around [48]
Rd 23	*(SC in next 2sts, SC2tog, SC in next 2sts) from*rep x8 [40]
Rd 24	*(SC in next 3sts, SC2tog) from*rep x8 [32]
Rd 25	*(SC in next st, SC2tog, SC in next st) from*rep x8 [24]

Slimy Candy Corn

Rd 26	*(SC in next st, SC2tog) from*rep x8 [16]
	Stuff
Rd 27	SC2tog x8 [8]
	Cut off thread and sew the opening

ARMs make x2 (work in continuous rounds)

Rd 1	**Wheat:** 5SC in magic ring [5] tighten the ring
Rd 2	INC in each st around [10]
Rd 3-5	SC in each st around [10] Change to Bright Yellow I last st. Cut off Wheat
Rd 6-10	**Bright Yellow:** SC in each st around [10] Change to White in last st. Cut off Bright Yellow
Rd 11-17	**White:** SC in each st around [10]

Cut off thread leaving a long tail for sewing

NOSE (work in continuous rounds)

Rd 1	**Wheat:** 6SC in magic ring [6] tighten the ring
Rd 2	INC in each st around [12]
Rd 3	*(SC in next st, INC in next st) from*rep x6 [18]
Rd 4-5	SC in each st around [18]
Rd 6	*(SC in next st, SC2tog) from*rep x6 [12]

Cut off thread leaving a long tail for sewing. Stuff the nose a bit

MUSTACHE x2 (work in continuous rounds)

Rd 1	**White:** 4SC in magic ring [4] tighten the ring
Rd 2	*(SC in next st, INC in next st) from*rep x2 [6]
Rd 3	INC in each of next 2sts, SC in next 4sts [8]
Rd 4	SC in next st, INC in each of next 2sts, SC in next 5sts [10]
Rd 5-8	SC in each st around [10]
Rd 9	SC2tog x5 [5]

Cut off thread leaving a long tail for sewing.

BOOTs x2 (work in continuous rounds)

Rd 1	**Black:** 6SC in magic ring [6] tighten the ring
Rd 2	INC each st around [12]
Rd 3	*(SC in next st, INC in next st) from*rep x6 [18]
Rd 4-6	SC in each st around [18]
Rd 7	*(SC in next st, SC2tog) from*rep x6 [12]

Fold in half, stuff and stitch edges of the opening together by SC (SC in 6sts). Cut off thread leaving a long tail for sewing.

DROP

Rd 1	**Light green:** In magic ring: 3SC, Ch2, sl st in 2nd st from hook, 3SC. Tighten the ring

Cut off thread leaving a long tail for sewing.

How to make a neat edge: https://youtu.be/5mqkO3leGoI

Sew the mustache on the body under the hat brim in front (4 stitches FLO).
Sew or glue the nose above the mustache.
Sew the arms on the body on sides (4 stitches FLO for each arm)
Sew the boots on the Rd 21 of the body.
Sew or glue the small drop on the body. Make the twisted cord with White and Violet (page 13)

An exciting world of crochet gnomres

CROCHET GNOMES

More crochet gnomes patterns,
inspiration, social media
Find here

SCAN
ME

Printed in Great Britain
by Amazon

26826462R00064